FABER EARLY ORGAN SERIE

European Organ Music of the 16th & 17th Cen
Series Editor : James Dalton

Volume 2

England

1590-1650

BYRD · WEELKES · O.GIBBONS · BULL
BROWN · COSYN · TOMKINS · PORTMAN

EDITED BY
GEOFFREY COX

Faber Music Limited

London

© 1986 by Faber Music Ltd
First published in 1986 by Faber Music Ltd
3 Queen Square London WC1N 3AU
Music engraved by Christopher Hinkins
Typeset by Goodfellow & Egan, Cambridge
Cover design by M & S Tucker
Cover illustration by John Brennan
German translations by Ursula Riniker
Printed in England by J. B. Offset Printers (Marks Tey) Ltd
All rights reserved

The facsimile on page x is reproduced by
permission of the British Library, London.

Contents – Inhalt

Editorial Procedure

This is a practical performing edition. All the pieces are presented in modern staff notation using treble and bass clefs. Within this arrangement, as much information as possible about the original sources is included on the score – considerably more, in some cases, than is found in other modern editions. The result, however, is not a facsimile in easy clefs; the editorial method that has been evolved is summarised as follows:

1. Unless otherwise indicated, original note-values, bar-lines, key-signatures and time-signatures have been preserved, and the distribution of notes between the staves retained. (In final chords, original note-values have been preserved even where not every part has the same number of beats.) Owing to the use of modern staves and clefs, original stem directions have sometimes been altered, but an attempt has been made to retain the idiomatic free-voiced appearance of the original keyboard notation.

2. Original clefs and notation are indicated at the beginning of each piece, and at other points where necessary. Where a time-signature or proportion-sign occurring in the course of a piece has been altered, the original is shown between the staves.

3. Where unusual notation (e.g. black semibreves, white demi-semi-minims) appears in the original, it has been changed to a modern equivalent and noted in the Critical Commentary.

4. Note-values extending over bar-lines have been transcribed using ties; otherwise, original note-groupings (unconventional beaming of quavers included) have generally been preserved. Although this can produce the appearance of inconsistency, there is often a purpose to the original script, and alteration in some cases but not in others would produce a confused picture. The only exceptions concern early sources in which each quaver or semiquaver has a separate tail, for which a straightforward, conventional routine (for example, beaming semiquavers in groups of four) has been employed.

5. Accidentals have been reproduced in full as they occur in the sources, except that, where applicable, sharps and flats have been replaced by modern naturals (for example, f♮ is often given as f♭ in the original, and b♮ as b♯). Normally, an original accidental applies to only one note and immediate repetitions of it; where it appears to hold good for longer than this, no cancelling accidental has been added, and the modern convention of an accidental being effective for the remainder of the bar applies (the same convention applies in the case of accidentals supplied editorially). All editorial accidentals are given at full size in square brackets. Some are essential because of the different conventions governing old and modern notation, while others are suggestions; the types can be distinguished by context.

6. Editorial ornaments, notes, rests and other details are given in square brackets. Ties added editorially are shown as ⌒. Editorial bar-lines are left unjoined between the staves, while in the occasional case of re-barring the original bar-lines are given in heavy type above the stave. The interpolation of a longer or shorter bar should not be seen as invalidating the underlying rhythmic flow. Original indications of part-movement have been retained; editorial indications are shown by broken lines.

7. For any piece appearing in more than one source, a main source has been chosen. It appears at the top of the list of sources for that piece in the Critical Commentary, and its text is regarded as basic. Any deviations from it (where, for instance, corrections have been made by the editor or where another source provides for superior reading) are noted in the Commentary. No attempt has been made to provide an exhaustive list of variants in additional sources.

8. A title has been provided at the head of each piece. Where titles and ascriptions are given in the sources, they are noted, in their original spellings, in the Commentary.

Introduction

With the accession of Elizabeth to the English throne in 1558 and the suppression of the Latin rite, the chant-based music that had played such a prominent part in the English organ repertory lost its strictly liturgical function and the role of the organ became less clearly defined. Some of its new functions may nonetheless have evolved from earlier practices. At Lincoln in 1570, for example, William Byrd was instructed to play the organ before the chanting of the canticles at both Morning and Evening Prayer,[1] a use that may be related to the organ settings of proper antiphons to the canticles (such as *Clarifica me Pater* and *Lucem tuam*) before the Reformation. At Ludlow it was agreed in 1581 that as well as accompanying the choir, the organ should be played 'betwine the psalms'.[2] An instruction issued by the Dean and Chapter of Chichester on 27 September 1616 also suggests an association of organ music with psalms: it refers to the use of the organ between the psalms and the first lesson,[3] and this may similarly be related to pre-Reformation organ settings of psalm antiphons such as *Miserere*. In the early seventeenth century, the Chapel Royal organ was played during formal arrivals and departures, and it was often referred to as playing an 'offertorye'.[4]

It is not known whether chant-based organ music was used for these purposes after the Reformation, but the similarity of some of these uses to older ones may partially explain the continuing tradition of writing such music. However, it is clear that composers of both keyboard and consort music also continued to write settings of plainchant as compositional exercises. This is evident in the tradition of pieces entitled 'In nomine' and based on the chant *Gloria tibi Trinitas* (see Vol. 1, Introduction). The settings of

this chant by John Bull (c1563–1628), of which one is included here, can be dated before 1613 when he left England for the Netherlands. There is no indication that they were intended specifically for the organ and, like most other keyboard music of this period, they could equally well be performed on the harpsichord or virginals.

The organ also developed entirely new roles after the Reformation. A work of 1611 by Edward Gibbons of Exeter is described as 'A Prelude upon ye Organ, as was then usuall before ye Anthem',[5] implying that organ music was customary (in Exeter at least) before the anthem at Morning and Evening Prayer. The two shortest pieces in this volume may have been written with such a function in mind. The Short Preludio of Four Parts by Orlando Gibbons (1583–1625) is concise enough not to detract from whatever music might follow. The Toccata by William Brown could equally be described as an *intonazione* in the Italian style.

One obvious outcome of the less clearly defined role of the organ in the liturgy was that composers were encouraged to write organ music that was not based on chant, and the freely imitative forms entered a period of tremendous growth in England. Variously entitled 'fancies', 'fantasias', 'verses' or 'voluntaries', they all answer to Thomas Morley's description of the fantasy as a piece in which 'a musician taketh a point at his pleasure, and wresteth and turneth it as he list, making either much or little of it according as shall seeme best in his own conceit'.[6] Lacking a fully developed native tradition in this type of music, it seems likely that English composers at the time looked to foreign models. It is significant that Antonio de Cabezón, the greatest Spanish keyboard composer of his day, spent more than a year in England (1554–5) in his capacity as court organist to Phillip II of Spain. The fantasias and voluntaries of William Byrd (c1543–1623) and others may have been modelled on his *tientos*, some of which were published in 1557 and 1578.[7]

The Fancy by Byrd included here is typical of his work in its succession of sections in varied styles, ranging from the strictly contrapuntal opening to quasi-antiphonal block chords (bar 30) and free-voiced keyboard texture later in the piece. Other composers, among them Orlando Gibbons and Thomas Tomkins (1572–1656), preferred a more consistently contrapuntal approach, derived perhaps from the tradition of the string fantasia but also eminently suited to the organ.[8] The influence of the Italian canzona with its lively rhythms and repeated-note themes is evident in such pieces as Gibbons's Fancy in C fa ut and Tomkins's Verse, while the ricercar style is suggested by the slower-moving themes of Tomkins's Fantasy and Gibbons's Fancy in Gamut flatt.

Of the two short voluntaries by Thomas Weelkes (c1576–1623), only the second is ascribed to 'Mr. Wilkes' in one of the sources (see Critical Commentary); however, they appear together in this source, and the ascription has been taken to refer to both pieces. The two anonymous three-part voluntaries and the one attributed here to Benjamin Cosyn (c1570–c1652) all come from a manuscript compiled by the mid-seventeenth century Oxford scribe and organist William Ellis (see Critical Commentary). The ascription

to 'B.C.' which appears after eight pieces in this manuscript must, however, be treated with some caution as one of the pieces so ascribed is known to be by Orlando Gibbons, and another is written in a style earlier than might be expected for Cosyn (see Vol. I No. 7).

The Verse for Double Organ by Richard Portman (d c1655) is one of the few pieces of the period in which the organ, as distinct from the virginals, is clearly specified. 'Double' here refers to an organ with two manuals, generally designated 'Great' and 'Chair'. In the typical double-organ voluntary of the period, the left hand is given a series of intermittent solos on the Great Organ, while the right hand plays continuously on the Chair Organ. The two hands normally play together on the Great at the end. Portman's piece owes something to French influence; according to Anthony Wood, he 'travel'd into France with Dr. John Williams Deane of Westminster',[9] and Thomas Ford's biographical notes add that he was 'advanced to the K[in]g's Chappel at his return'.[10] The latter part of Portman's piece reflects the influence of the French *dialogue à deux choeurs* style in which both hands alternate simultaneously between the two manuals. Later, this style was to find a further, tentative application in the double-organ voluntaries of Christopher Gibbons and Matthew Locke.

Geoffrey Cox
Melbourne, 1986

1 W. Shaw: 'William Byrd of Lincoln', *Music and Letters*, xlviii (1967), pp.56–7

2 A. Smith: 'Elizabethan Church Music at Ludlow', *Music and Letters*, xlix (1968), pp.113–4

3 J. H. Steele: *English Organs and Organ Music from 1500 to 1650* (unpublished PhD diss., Cambridge, 1958–9), p.243

4 E. F. Rimbault: *The Old Cheque-Book . . . of the Chapel Royal, from 1561 to 1744* (London: Camden Society, 1872), pp.150, 159, 167–9

5 British Library, London, MS Harl. 7340, f.193v

6 T. Morley: *A Plaine and Easie Introduction to Practicall Musicke* (London, 1597), p.181

7 S. Kastner: 'Parallels and Discrepancies between English and Spanish Keyboard Music of the Sixteenth and Seventeenth Century', *Anuario musical*, vii (1952), pp.77–115

8 The opening point of the first anonymous voluntary (p.24) is identical with that of a Fantasy à 3 for strings by Coprario (Charteris No. 11, Meyer No. 7).

9 Bodleian Library, Oxford, MS Wood D.19 (4), f.103v

10 Bodleian Library, Oxford, MS Mus.e.17, f.39

Ornamentation

The main ornament signs used by sixteenth- and early seventeenth-century English composers are single and double strokes: ♪ , ♪ , etc. and ♪ , ♪ , etc. In the absence of any unequivocal explanations in contemporary sources, ♪ might be interpreted as ♫ or, less likely, as ♫ [11]; while ♪ most probably indicates a trill or

short shake – ♫ – or possibly ♫ in some contexts.[12]

The ornamentation in Portman's Verse for Double Organ, though idiosyncratically notated, is of the later style used after the Restoration. The four signs used by Portman are as follows (full details are given in Vol. 3):

	Sign	Interpretation
Forefall		
Shake		
Backfall and Shake		
Shake Turned		

11 This interpretation of the single-stroke ornament is suggested in a table of ornaments attributed to Elway Bevin and dating from c1630 in British Library Add. MS 31403.

12 For more detailed discussion of single- and double-stroke ornaments, see P. G. le Huray: 'English Keyboard Fingering', in I. Bent, ed.: *Source Materials and the Interpretation of Music* (London: Stainer & Bell, 1981), pp.251–7.

Registration

Owing to the lack of instruments and documentary sources, any suggestions for registration in sixteenth-century English organ music must be general rather than specific. Anthony Duddyngton's contract of 1519[13] is puzzling and inconsistent, but it is the fullest and most informative document of its kind to survive from the period. The compass of the manual described by Duddyngton runs from C to a" ('xxvii playne keyes'), and the pitch is probably about a major third below the present-day level ('x foot or more'). While some of the ranks can be drawn at will ('as fewe stops as may be convenient'), there is most probably a *Blokwerk* type of chorus which cannot be divided up into separate registers.[14]

There are several instances in this anthology where the upper limit of Duddyngton's keyboard (a") is exceeded, while the lowest part does not go down below c. Such passages may have been intended for the Principal (without the 'Bassys called Diapason'), implying performance an octave lower than written, but at 4' pitch; verses 1, 3, and 7 of the anonymous *Magnificat* included in Volume 1, where the direction 'play bothe parts viii nots lower heer' occurs, are a case in point. While such pieces appear to be for a low-pitched organ (a view supported by the vocal range of the plainchant, which can be uncomfortably high unless transposed down), others may be intended for the English fifteenth-century organ, based on F and sounding approximately a minor 3rd above present-day pitch,[15] that continued in use throughout the sixteenth century. Preston's *Benedictus sit Deus Pater* (Vol. 1 No. 6), for example, does not descend below F, and its *cantus firmus* would probably have sounded a minor third above written pitch when sung.

Activity in organ-building declined after the Reformation, but the appearance of 'newe double organs' in the Jacobean period marks a resurgence. Thomas Tomkins played on a two-manual organ built for Worcester Cathedral by Thomas Dallam in 1613. The treasurer's accounts in Worcester Cathedral Library[16] include the following description: '... the particulars of the great organ. / Two open diapasons of metall / CC fa ut a pipe of 10 foot long / Two principals of metal / Two small principals or 15ths of metal / One twelfth of mettall / One recorder of mettal, a stopt pipe / In the Chair Organ / One principal of mettal / One diapason of wood / One flute of wood / One small principal or fifteenth of mettal / One two and twentieth of mettal.'

It is possible that the early 'double organ' was a combination of the previous high-pitched and low-pitched instruments, in which case there could be no question of the manuals being intended for use together. From the fact that the great CC-fa-ut needed 'a pipe 10 foot long', it seems that sixteenth-century low pitch was still in use, for this manual at least, and some of Tomkins's music may be intended to sound at a lower pitch than present-day level.

Registration for most of this music can be limited to one or two stops, based on 8' tone, with full registrations being reserved for special occasions. Reeds, mixtures and 16' stops are not appropriate.

---

13 Given in Hopkins & Rimbault: *The Organ: its History and Construction* (3rd edn., London: Robert Cocks, 1877/R1965), pp.56-7, and in facsimile in P.R.W. Blewett: *Anthony Duddyngton, Organ Maker* (London, 1977).

14 Problems of pitch are therefore at least as great as those of registration in performing this repertory, although transposition in modern performances runs many dangers, among them contending with the physical difficulties of a strange key, problems of fingering and even of tuning and temperament.

15 See J. Caldwell: 'The Pitch of Early Tudor Organ Music', *Music and Letters*, li (1970), pp.156–63.

16 MS d. 248

Anmerkung des Herausgebers

Die vorliegende Ausgabe richtet sich an praktizierende Musiker. Alle Musikstücke erscheinen in moderner Liniennotation unter Verwendung von Violin- und Baßschlüsseln. Die Partituren dieser Ausgabe enthalten so viel Information wie möglich über die Originalquellen – in einigen Fällen bedeutend mehr, als in anderen modernen Ausgaben zu finden ist. Das Resultat ist jedoch nicht eine vereinfachte Reproduktion des Originals. Eine systematische Methode der Herausgabe wurde entwickelt, die im Folgenden zusammengefaßt wird:

1. Wenn nicht anders vermerkt, sind die Notenwerte, Taktstriche, Tonart- und Taktvorzeichen des Originals beibehalten worden, ebenso die Verteilung der Noten zwischen den Linien. (In Schlußakkorden sind die Notenwerte des Originals beibehalten worden, auch da, wo nicht jede Stimme die gleiche Anzahl Schläge zählt.) Wegen der neuzeitlichen Notenlinien und Schlüssel ist die Richtung der Notenhälse manchmal geändert worden, doch hat man versucht, die idiomatische freie Notation des Originals beizubehalten. Mehrstimmige Partituren sind auf zwei Systeme umgeschrieben worden.

2. Die Original-Notenschlüssel und/oder -Notationen sind am Anfang von jedem Stück vermerkt, und auch anderswo, wenn nötig. Wo ein Taktvorzeichen oder eine Mensuralnotation mitten im Stück abgeändert worden ist, erscheint das Originalzeichen zwischen den Systemen.

3. Wo im Original ungewöhnliche Notation auftritt (z.B. schwarze ganze Noten, weiße Achtelnoten) ist die entsprechende moderne Notation verwendet und im kritischen Kommentar erwähnt worden.

4. Notenwerte, die sich über Taktstriche hinaus erstrecken, sind unter der Verwendung von Haltebögen umgeschrieben worden; im übrigen sind die Notengruppierungen des Originals (einschließlich unkonventionellen Verbindens von Achtelnoten mit Balken) beibehalten worden. Trotz dieser scheinbaren Inkonsequenz ist die Originalnotation nicht unbegründet, und eine Abänderung würde in gewissen, wenn auch nicht in allen Fällen zur Verwirrung führen. Die einzigen Ausnahmen sind frühe Quellen, wo jede Achtelnote oder Sechzehntelnote ein separates Fähnchen aufweist. Hier ist eine klare konventionelle Notation verwendet worden (z.B. das Verbinden von Sechzehntelnoten mit Balken in Vierergruppen).

5. In den Quellen enthaltene Vorzeichen sind unverändert übernommen worden, mit der Ausnahme, daß allfällig Erhöhungs- und Erniedrigungszeichen durch moderne Notation ersetz worden sind (z.B. erscheint f♮ im Original oft als f♭, und e♮ als e♯). Normalerweise gilt ein Vorzeichen im Original nur für eine Note und gleich darauf folgende Wiederholungen; wo es länger zu gelten scheint, gilt ohne Vermerk des Herausgebers die heutige Konvention, wonach ein Vorzeichen für den Rest des Taktes in Kraft bleibt. (Die gleiche Regel gilt für Vorzeichen, die vom Herausgeber hinzugefügt wurden.) Alle Vorzeichen des Herausgebers sind in voller Größe in eckigen Klammern gegeben. Einige vom Herausgeber hinzugefügte Vorzeichen sind infolge der verschiedenen Konventionen der alten und modernen Notation, unumgänglich, während andere als Anregungen betrachtet werden sollten. Die zwei Arten sind aus dem Zusammenhang ersichtlich.

6. Vom Herausgeber hinzugefügte Verzierungen, Noten, Pausen

und andere Einzelheiten befinden sich in eckigen Klammern. Vom Herausgeber beigefügte Haltebögen erscheinen wie folgt: ⌒. Taktstriche des Herausgebers sind zwischen den Systemen unverbunden, während bei gelegentlichem neuen Einsetzen von Taktstrichen die Originaltaktstriche in Fettdruck über den Systemen erscheinen. Das Einsetzen eines längeren oder kürzeren Taktes hat nicht die Absicht, den zugrunde liegenden rhythmischen Ablauf zu verändern. Hinweise auf den Verlauf der Stimmen im Original sind beibehalten worden; Zusätze des Herausgebers verwenden gestrichelte Linien.

7. Für jedes Werk, das in mehr als einer Quelle erscheint, wurde eine Hauptquelle gewählt. Sie erscheint am Anfang der Liste der Quellen für das betreffende Stück im kritischen Kommentar, und diese Version wird als Grundlage betrachtet. Allfällige Abweichungen von der Hauptquelle (z.B. wo vom Herausgeber Korrekturen angebracht wurden oder wo stellenweise eine andere Quelle vorgezogen wurde) sind im Kommentar vermerkt. Wir haben keinen Versuch unternommen, eine erschöpfende Liste von Varianten in anderen Quellen zu erstellen.

8. Jedes Werk ist mit einer Überschrift versehen worden. Wo Überschriften und Zuschreibungen in den Quellen enthalten sind, sind sie in der Schreibweise des Originals im Kommentar erwähnt.

Vorwort

Mit der Thronbesteigung von Elizabeth in England im Jahre 1558 und der Unterdrückung des lateinischen Ritus verlor die auf den gregorianischen Gesang gestützte Musik, die im englischen Orgelrepertoire eine so große Rolle gespielt hatte, ihre strikt liturgische Funktion, und die Rolle der Orgel war nun weniger genau umgrenzt. Einige ihrer neuen Funktionen dürften sich trotzdem aus der früheren Tradition entwickelt haben. Im Jahre 1570 in Lincoln zum Beispiel hatte William Byrd die Aufgabe, vor dem Singen der Lobgesänge sowohl bei der Mette als auch bei der Vesper die Orgel zu spielen[1], ein Brauch, der mit den Orgelbearbeitungen spezieller Antiphonen zu den Lobgesängen (wies z.B. *Clarifica me Pater* und *Lucem tuam*) vor der Reformation in Beziehung stehen dürfte. In Ludlow vereinbarte man 1581, daß die Orgel nicht nur den Chor begleiten, sondern auch zwischen den Psalmen spielen sollte.[2] Eine vom Dekan und Kapitel von Chichester am 27. September 1616 erlassene Weisung verbindet ebenfalls die Orgelmusik mit den Psalmen. Sie bezieht sich auf die Verwendung der Orgel zwischen den Psalmen und der ersten Lesung,[3] und dies dürfte analog zu Orgelbearbeitungen von Psalm-Antiphonen wie des *Miserere* vor der Reformation in Beziehung stehen. Im frühen 17. Jahrhundert spielte die Orgel der königlichen Kapelle bei formellen Ankünften und Abgängen, und es hieß oft, man spiele ein Offertorium.[4]

Wir wissen nicht, ob auf den Choral gestützte Orgelmusik nach der Reformation zu diesem Zweck verwendet wurde, doch die Ähnlichkeit einiger neuerer Funktionen der Orgel mit älteren dürfte teilweise erklären, warum die Tradition im Komponieren solcher Musik fortgesetzt wurde. Allerdings besteht kein Zweifel, daß Komponisten sowohl von Tastenmusik als auch von Ensemblemusik auch weiter Bearbeitungen von cantus planus als Kompositionsübungen schrieben. Dies zeigt sich in der Tradition von Werken mit dem Titel 'In nomine', die sich auf den Choral *Gloria tibi Trinitas* (vgl. Band 1, Vorwort) stützen. Die Bearbeitungen dieses Chorals von John Bull (ca. 1563–1628), von denen eine hier vorliegt, stammen aus der Zeit vor 1613, als er England verließ und nach Holland reiste. Es gibt keine Hinweise dafür, daß diese Bearbeitungen speziell für die Orgel bestimmt waren, und wie die meiste Tastenmusik jener Zeit konnten sie ebenso gut auf dem Cembalo oder Virginal gespielt werden.

Nach der Reformation bekam die Orgel auch ganz neue Funktionen. Ein Werk von 1611 von Edward Gibbons von Exeter wird wie folgt beschrieben: 'Ein Vorspiel auf der Orgel, wie es damals vor dem Chorgesang üblich war',[5] was darauf hinweist, daß Orgelmusik (zumindest in Exeter) bei der Mette und Vesper vor dem Chorgesang üblich war. Die zwei kürzesten Stücke im vorliegenden Band dürften zu diesem Zweck komponiert worden sein. Das *Short Preludio of Four Parts* von Orlando Gibbons (1583–1625) ist nicht lang genug, um von der darauf folgenden Musik abzulenken. Die Toccata von William Brown könnte ebenso gut als *intonazione* im italienischen Stil bezeichnet werden.

Eine eindeutige Folge der weniger klar umgrenzten Rolle der Orgel in der Liturgie war, daß die Komponisten dazu ermuntert wurden, Orgelmusik zu schreiben, die nicht auf liturgischen Gesängen beruhte, und die frei imitierenden Kompositionen erlebten eine Blütezeit in England. Sie sind je nachdem als 'fancies', 'fantasias', 'verses' oder 'voluntaries' bezeichnet, und Thomas Morleys Beschreibung der Fantasie als ein Stück, in dem 'ein Musiker eine Idee nach Belieben wählt und sie dreht und wendet und entweder viel oder wenig daraus macht, wie es ihm am besten erscheint',[6] trifft auf alle zu. Da eine voll entwickelte einheimische Tradition in dieser Musikart fehlte, haben sich englische Komponisten damals wahrscheinlich nach ausländischen Vorbildern gerichtet. Es ist bezeichnend, daß Antonio de Cabezón, seinerzeit der größte spanische Komponist von Tastenmusik, mehr als ein Jahr (1554–5) in England verbrachte als Hoforganist Philips II. von Spanien. Die *fantasias* und *voluntaries* von William Byrd (ca. 1543–1623) und anderen dürften sich an Cabezóns *tientos* anlehnen, von denen einige 1557 und 1578 veröffentlicht wurden.[7]

Die hier vorliegende *Fancy* ist charakteristisch für Byrds Kompositionen mit ihrer Folge von unterschiedlichen Stilarten, vom strikt kontrapunktischen Anfang zu quasi-antiphonalen Blockakkorden (Takt 30) und frei intonierter Tastenmusik später im gleichen Stück. Andere Komponisten, u.a. Orlando Gibbons und Thomas Tomkins (1572–1656), zogen einen konsequenteren kontrapunktischen Stil vor, der sich möglicherweise an die Tradition der Fantasia für Streichinstrumente anlehnte, der aber auch für die Orgel bestens geeignet war.[8] Der Einfluß der italienischen canzona mit ihren lebhaften Rhythmen und thematischen Wiederholungen zeigt sich in Werken wie Gibbons *Fancy in C fa ut* und Tomkins' *Verse*, während das ricercar in den langsameren Melodien in Tomkins' *Fantasy* und Gibbons *Fancy in Gamut flatt* zum Vorschein kommt.

Von den zwei kurzen *Voluntaries* von Thomas Weelkes (ca. 1576–1623) ist nur das zweite in einer der Quellen 'Mr Wilkes' zugeschrieben (vgl. kritischer Kommentar). Sie erscheinen jedoch zusammen in jener Quelle, und es wird vermutet, daß sich die Zuschreibung auf beide Stücke bezieht. Die beiden anonymen dreistimmigen *Voluntaries* und das hier Benjamin Cosyn (ca. 1570–ca. 1652) zugeschriebene sind einem Manuskript entnommen, das der Oxford Kopist und Organist William Ellis zusammengestellt hat (vgl. kritischer Kommentar). Die Zuschreibung 'B.C.', die nach acht Stücken in diesem Manuskript erscheint, muß jedoch mit Vorbehalt betrachtet werden, da eines der so bezeichneten Werke bekanntlich von Orlando Gibbons stammt, und ein anderes ist in einem früheren Stil geschrieben, als man es von Cosyn erwarten würde (s. Band I, Nr. 7).

Das *Verse for Double Organ* von Richard Portman (gest. ca. 1655) ist eines der wenigen Stücke jener Zeit, in denen die Orgel im Gegensatz zum Virginal deutlich genannt wird. 'Doppel' (*Double*) bezieht sich hier auf eine Orgel mit zwei Manualen, allgemein als Hauptmanual (*Great Organ*) und Rückpositiv (*Chair Organ*) bezeichnet. Im typischen *voluntary* jener Zeit für Doppelorgel spielt die linke Hand periodisch Solos auf dem Hauptmanual, während die rechte Hand ununterbrochen auf dem Rückpositiv spielt. Beide Hände spielen normalerweise am Ende zusammen auf dem Hauptmanual. Portmans Werk weist französische Einflüsse auf; nach Anthony Wood 'reiste er nach Frankreich mit Dr. John Williams, Dekan von Westminster'[9], und in Thomas Fords biographischen Notizen steht, daß er 'nach seiner Rückkehr zur königlichen Kapelle aufstieg'[10]. Der letztere Teil von Portmans Werk zeigt den Einfluß des französischen *dialogue à deux choeurs* – Stils, in dem beide Hände gleichzeitig zwischen den zwei Manualen abwechseln. Später sollte dieser Stil eine weitere versuchsweise Anwendung finden in den *voluntaries* für Doppelorgel von Christopher Gibbons und Matthew Locke.

Geoffrey Cox
Melbourne, 1986

1 W. Shaw: 'William Byrd of Lincoln', *Music and Letters*, xlviii (1967), S.56–7
2 A. Smith: 'Elizabethan Church Music at Ludlow', *Music and Letters*, xlix (1968), S.113–14

3 J. H. Steele: *English Organs and Organ Music from 1500 to 1650* (unveröffentlichte Dissertation, Cambridge, 1958–9), S.243
4 E. F. Rimbault: *The Old Cheque-Book ... of the Chapel Royal, from 1561 to 1744* (London: Camden Society, 1872), S.150, 159, 167–9
5 British Library, London, MS Harl. 7340, f.193v
6 T. Morley: *A Plaine and Easie Introduction to Practicall Musicke* (London, 1597), S.181
7 S.Kastner: 'Parallels and Discrepancies between English and Spanish Keyboard Music of the Sixteenth and Seventeenth Century', *Anuario musical*, vii (1952), S.77–115
8 Der Teil am Anfang der ersten anonymen *Voluntary* (S.24) ist übereinstimmend mit dem einer *Fantasy à 3* von Coprario (Charteris Nr. 11; Meyer Nr. 7).
9 Bodleian Library, Oxford, MS Wood D.19 (4), f.103v
10 Bodleian Library, Oxford, MS Mus.e.17, f.39

Ornamentierung

Die wichtigsten Ornamentierungszeichen, die von englischen Komponisten des 16. und frühen 17. Jahrhunderts verwendet wurden, sind Einzel- und Doppelstriche ⌀ , ♩ , etc. und ⸙ , ♯ , etc. Mangels eindeutiger Erklärungen in zeitgenössischen Quellen, könnte ♩ als ♫ oder, nicht so wahrscheinlich, als ♫♩[11] interpretiert werden, während ♯ höchst wahrscheinlich einen langen Triller oder Pralltriller darstellt – ♫♩ – oder vielleicht ♫♩ in manchen Kontexten.[12]

Die Ornamentierung in Portmans *Verse for Double Organ* gehört, obwohl individuell aufgezeichnet, dem späteren, nach der Restauration gebräuchlichen Stil an. Die vier von Portman verwendeten Zeichen sind die folgenden (genauere Angaben befinden sich im dritten Band):

	Zeichen	Interpretation
Appoggiatura		
Triller		
Vorschlag von oben und Triller		
Triller mit Nachschlag		

11 Diese Interpretation der Einzelstrich-Ornamentierung ist in einer Elway Bevin (ca. 1630) zugeschriebenen Ornamentierungstabelle in der British Library, Add. MS 31403, enthalten.
12 Für eine eingehendere Diskussion der Einzel- und Doppelstrich-Ornamentierungen siehe P. G. le Huray: 'English Keyboard Fingering', in I. Bent, Herausgeber: *Source Materials and the Interpretation of Music* (London: Stainer & Bell, 1981), S.251–7.

Registrierung

Infolge des Mangels an Instrumenten und dokumentarischen Quellen ist jeglicher Hinweis auf Registrierung in englischer Orgelmusik des 16. Jahrhunderts eher allgemeiner als spezifischer Natur. Anthony Duddyngtons Abhandlung von 1519[13] ist rätselhaft und widersprüchlich, ist jedoch das vollständigste und aufschlußreichste Dokument seiner Art, das uns aus jener Zeit erhalten geblieben ist. Der von Duddyngton beschriebene Manualumfang verläuft von C bis a" ('xxvii playne keyes'), und die Tonhöhe ist vermutlich etwa um eine Dur-Terz unter der heutigen Tonlage ('x foot or more'). Während einige der Register beliebig gezogen werden können ('so wenige Register wie gewünscht'), gibt es höchst wahrscheinlich einen Blockwerk Chor, der nicht in einzelne Register aufgeteilt werden kann.[14]

Diese Anthologie enthält einige Beispiele, wo die obere Grenze von Duddyngtons Tastatur (a") überschritten wird, während die tiefste Stimme nicht unter c geht. Solche Stellen waren wohl für den Prinzipal (ohne die 'Diapason genannte Bassys') bestimmt, wobei die Tonlage um eine Oktave tiefer ist als notiert. Die 1., 3. und 7. Strophe des im 1. Band enthaltenen anonymen *Magnificat*'s mit der Anmerkung 'beide Stimmen sind hier acht Noten tiefer zu spielen' deuten darauf hin. Während solche Werke für eine Orgel mit niedriger Tonlage bestimmt zu sein scheinen (eine Ansicht, die vom Tonumfang des cantus planus bestätigt wird, der unangenehm hoch sein kann, wenn er nicht hinuntertransponiert wird), mögen andere für die englische Orgel des 15. Jahrhunderts geschrieben sein, mit F als Grundlage und etwa eine Moll-Terz höher als heute gespielt.[15] Diese Orgel wurde während des ganzen 16. Jahrhunderts weiter verwendet. Prestons *Benedictus sit Deus Pater* (1. Band, Nr. 6) zum Beispiel geht nicht tiefer als F, und sein *cantus firmus* wäre wohl eine Moll-Terz über der aufgezeichneten Tonlage gesungen worden.

Der Orgelbau nahm nach der Reformation ab, doch das Erscheinen neuer Doppelorgeln zur Zeit Jakobs I. bedeutet eine Wiederbelebung. Thomas Tomkins spielte auf einer Orgel mit zwei Manualen, die von Thomas Dallam 1613 für die Kathedrale von Worcester gebaut worden war. In den Büchern des Schatzmeisters in der Bibliothek der Kathedrale von Worcester[16] steht folgende Beschreibung: '... die Einzelheiten des Hauptwerks. / Zwei offene Diapasone aus Metall / CC fa ut eine Pfeife von 10' Länge / Zwei Prinzipale aus Metall / Zwei kleine Prinzipale oder Fünfzehnten aus Metall / Eine Zwölfte aus Metall / Ein Recorder aus Metall, eine gedackte Pfeife / Im Rückpositiv / Ein Prinzipal aus Metall / Ein Diapason aus Holz / Eine Flöte aus Holz / Ein kleiner Prinzipal oder eine Fünfzehnte aus Metall / Eine Zweiundzwanzigste aus Metall.'

Es ist möglich, daß die frühe Doppelorgel die vorhergegangenen Instrumente hoher und niedriger Tonlage in sich vereinte, wobei die Manuale mit Sicherheit nicht zusammen betätigt werden sollten. Die Tatsache, daß das Hauptwerk CC-fa-ut 'eine Pfeife von 10' Länge' benötigte, scheint darauf hinzudeuten, daß die niedrige Tonlage des 16. Jahrhunderts immer noch im Gebrauch war, zumindest für dieses Werk, und Tomkins' Musik dürfte z.T. für eine tiefere Tonlage bestimmt gewesen sein als die heutige.

Die Registrierung für den größten Teil dieser Musik kann sich auf ein oder zwei Register beschränken, auf den 8' Ton gestützt, mit voller Registrierung für besondere Gelegenheiten reserviert. Zungen, Mixturen und 16' Register gehören nicht dazu.

---

13 Erwähnt in Hopkins & Rimbault: *The Organ: its History and Construction* (3. Auflage, London: Robert Cocks, 1877/R1965), S.56-7, und im Faksimile, in P.R.W. Blewett: *Anthony Duddyngton, Organ Maker* (London, 1977).

14 Die Probleme der Tonhöhen sind deshalb mindestens genau so Groß. Wie jene der Registrierungen bei der Aufführung dieser Sammlung, obwohl die Transposition bei modernen Aufführungen viele Gefahren in sich birgt, unter ihnen die Auseinandersetzung mit den natürlichen Schwierigkeiten einer fremden Tonart, Probleme des Fingerstazes und sogar der Stimmung und des Temperaments.

15 Siehe J. Caldwell: 'The Pitch of Early Tudor Organ Music', *Music and Letters*, li (1970), S.156–63.

16 MS d. 248

O. Gibbons: Fancy in Gamut flatt

(British Library, London, Royal Music Library MS 32.l.4
'Cosyn's Virginal Book', f. 103v)

1. *A Fancy*

WILLIAM BYRD (c1543-1623)

4

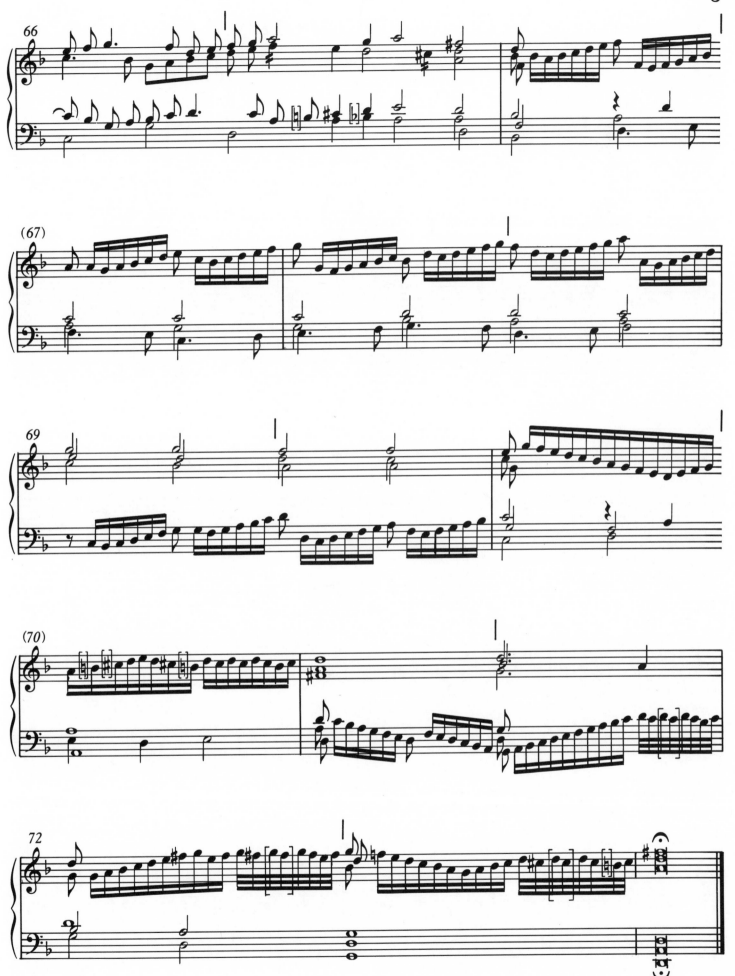

2. Two Voluntaries

THOMAS WEELKES *(c1575-1623)*

No.1

No.2

3. *A Fancy in C fa ut*

ORLANDO GIBBONS *(1583-1625)*

4. *A Fancy in Gamut flatt*

ORLANDO GIBBONS *(1583-1625)*

5. *A Short Preludio of Four Parts*

ORLANDO GIBBONS *(1583-1625)*

6. *Gloria tibi Trinitas*

JOHN BULL *(c1563-1628)*

7. *Toccata*

WILLIAM BROWN *(?d1637)*

8. *Voluntary*

BENJAMIN COSYN *(c1570-c1652)*

9. *Two Voluntaries*

ANONYMOUS *(early 17th century)*

No. 2

10. *Verse*

THOMAS TOMKINS *(1572-1656)*

11. *A Fantasy*

THOMAS TOMKINS *(1572-1656)*

12. *Verse for Double Organ*

RICHARD PORTMAN *(d c1655)*

*The ornaments are idiosyncratic, and have been reproduced as they appear in the source.
*Die Verzierungen sind charakteristisch und werden wie in der Quelle wiedergegeben.

Critical Commentary

Sources are listed for each piece, together with original titles and/or ascriptions where present. Where there is more than one source, the first listed represents the main source for the edition (see Editorial Procedure, §7); any deviations from the main source are detailed in the commentary below.

The following RISM sigla are used to indicate the libraries in which manuscripts are located:

    Lbl   – London: British Library
    Lcm – London: Royal College of Music
    NYp – New York: Public Library
    Och – Oxford: Christ Church Library
    Pc   – Paris: Bibliothéque du Conservatoire
    W   – Wimborne: Wimborne Minster Library

The following abbreviations are used:

    S   – soprano
    A   – alto
    T   – tenor
    B   – bass
    lh   – left hand
    rh   – right hand

Pitches are notated as follows:

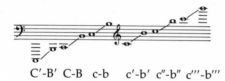

C'-B'   C-B   c-b   c'-b'   c"-b"   c'''-b'''

32 T 7–9 ♩ ♫ means that in bar 32 the seventh, eighth and ninth notes of the tenor part are a crotchet and two quavers in the source; 4 rh middle voice 2, 3 f'♯ g'♯ means that in bar 4, right hand, middle voice, the second and third notes are middle octave F♯ and G♯ in the source.

1. A Fancy

Lbl Add. MS 30485, f.103v. [untitled] *Mr Bird*
My Ladye Nevell's Book [privately owned], f.186v (No. 41). *A fancie; mr w Birde*
Bracketed notes, dots and accidentals at the following points are taken from *Nevell*: 8 lh 1; 49 A 7; 59 rh 24; 60 B 14; 66 T 10; 70 rh 18; 71 B 28–9; 72 rh 14–15 and 33–4.

14 A 4 d ♪ c ♪ in *Nevell* / 17 A 8 ♯ for f' in *Nevell* / 22 upper part 3–4 d" ♩. in *Lbl* / 26 rh 1 f"♩ in *Nevell* / 29 A 4–11 follows *Nevell*; *Lbl* has c' ♯ / 47 T 6–7 follows *Nevell*; *Lbl* has g♩d♩g♩ / 60 lh 1 d and f♯ ♩: in *Lbl*; ♩: in *Nevell* / 60 rh 4 ♮ for b in *Nevell*; b in *Lbl*

2. Two Voluntaries

NYp Drexel MS 5612, p.51. *Volluntarie 4 parts* [anon.] ⎤
Lcm MS 2093, ff.31v–30v. *A Voluntary* [anon.] ⎦ (No. 1)
25 B 1 ♯ for e in *NYp* / 39 A 2 ♯ for g' in *Lcm*

NYp Drexel MS 5612, p.52. *Voluntarie 4 parts Mr Wilkes* ⎤
Lcm MS 2093, ff.33-32. *A Voluntary* [anon.] ⎦ (No. 2)
28 A 2 ♯ for c' in *Lcm* / 34 A 4 ♯ for g' in *Lcm* / 43 A 1 ♯ for c' in *Lcm*

3. A Fancy in C fa ut

Lbl Royal Music Library MS 23.l.4 (Benjamin Cosyn), f.104v. *Fantasia; Or. Gibbons* [indexed as 'A fancy in C.fa.ut.']
Lbl Add. MS 31403, f.11v. *A Voluntary; Mr Orlando Gibbons*

Och MS 47, p.34. *Voluntarie of foure parts; Mr orlando Gibbons*
Och MS 1176, ff.8–7v. *Voluntarie of 4 parts; Mr orlando Gibbons*
The text in MS 1176 may have been copied from that in MS 47, or both may derive from a common source. These two sources contain bars 1–43 only, and end with a different cadence in bar 44. Variants in the secondary sources are not listed here in detail.
7 rh 2 ♩♩♪

4. A Fancy in Gamut flatt

Lbl Royal Music Library MS 23.l.4 (Benjamin Cosyn), f.103v. *Fantasia; Or. Gibbons* [indexed as 'A Fancy in Gamut flatt']
Cosyn began to arrange this piece for two manuals, but abandoned his attempt. The word *base* appears below lh in 15 and 23 and *ten[or]* above lh in 19.
34 B 1 B / 160 lh last note (upper part) a / 167 B 1 e

5. A Short Preludio of Four Parts

Lbl Add. MS 36661, f.44. *A Short Preludio of 4 parts; Mr Orlando Gibbons*
Och MS 1142(A), f.1. [untitled; anon.]
Fingering is from *Och*, a small amount of which also appears in *Lbl*.
4 T 1 f in rh in *Lbl*, but lh with fingering in *Och* / 7 B 4 – 8 B 1 additional f crotchets (tied)

6. Gloria tibi Trinitas

Pc MS Rés 1122, p.48. *gloria tibi Trinitas; doct. Bull*
The cantus firmus is undotted in 28–53, but the dotting is implied by the proportion sign; the other parts are in black notation.

7. Toccata

Och MS 89, p. 1. *Tocata ma Guil Bruno*
12 T 4 f♯

8. Voluntary

Och MS 1113, p.133 (No. 57). [untitled] *B.C.*
31 middle voice 4 b in both lh and rh.

9. Two Voluntaries

Och MS 1113, p.162 (No. 75). [untitled; anon.] (No. 1)
11 rh 1–20 rh 6 written a 3rd too low / 26 T 1 g
ibid., p.137 (No. 60). [untitled; anon.] (No. 2)
16 S 1 additional tie to previous c"♯

10. Verse

Och MS 1113, p.135 (No. 59). [untitled] *Mr Tho. Tomkins*
28 B 5 ♯ for f, possibly misplaced from c' in rh

11. A Fantasy

Pc MS Rés 1122, p.27. *A Fantasi; Tho. Tomkins 9ber. 1646: 9th* [in the composer's hand]
14 B 6 additional e ♩ / 45 rh lower voice 1–7 in lh / 37, 45, 47 notes in brackets supplied editorially; MS covered in ink here

12. Verse for Double Organ

W MS P.10, f.3v. *Verse for ye Double Organ; Mr Ric. Portman*
Single and *Double* denote Chair and Great respectively.
14 S 1 e" ○ / 30 lh 3 g' dotted / 40 rh 2 instruction *Double* is nearer the lh, but presumably applies to rh also / 44 A 1–6 in lh / 55 S 1 rest instead of a tied a" / 57 instruction *Double* given for both hands